Seville

Text by
FERNANDO OLMEDO

EDICIONES
Aldeasa

Seville

Short history

Seville is located on the banks of the Guadalquivir River, some eighty kilometers from where it joins the Atlantic. It is the capital of the Autonomous Community of Andalusia and the fourth most inhabited city in Spain with a population of about seven hundred thousand people. The city enjoys a benign and mild climate, with around 550 ml of annual rainfall between autumn and spring, close to 3.000 hours of sunlight a year and average temperatures of around 26° C in the summer months, and 12° C in the winter. Temperature lows seldom reach 0° C, while highs can reach 40° C in mid-summer.

Cheerful, passionate, self-assured and hospitable, loaded with history and yet modern at the same time, it is a destination of universal resonance combining a virtually unequaled monumental heritage with a baroque personality that is seen in the city's streets and traditions, reflecting both its attractive and clichéd characteristics. The result is a city that has been able to reconcile the present and the past, preserving its identity and keeping its traditions alive, something that can be seen in the spectacular celebrations that take place during Semana Santa (Holy Week) and the Feria de Abril, the Spring festival for which the city is renowned.

Guadalquivir River.

Azulejos depicting la Giralda

The ancient Hispalis

The origins of Seville can be traced back to the 8th century BC, when its roots were laid between the arms of the Guadalquivir River. Although mythology attributes the founding of the city to Hercules, archeological findings and the city's primitive name – Hispalis – link its origins to the Phoenicians. Favored for its position at the junction of important land and maritime routes, it was one of the enclaves of the legendary kingdom of Tartessos, famous in Antiquity for the richness of its mines and livestock. Hispalis consolidated its ascent starting in the 3rd century BC under Roman rule. Its river port turned it into a commercial trading center that exported minerals from the Sierra Morena Mountains as well as the copious agricultural production – oil, wine, and wheat – from the Guadalquivir Valley. In the year 45 BC, Julius Caesar confirmed its rank by giving it the title of *Colonia Iulia Romula*. The city of Itálica was established nearby. Of more selective lineage, it was the birthplace of the Emperors Trajan and Hadrian. Its ruins – once known as "The Old Seville" – are some of the best examples of the Roman legacy in Spain. During the reign of the Visigoths, the Sevillian capital retained its economic, political, and cultural importance, sheltering such notable figures as the wise San Isidro.

Muslim and Christian Seville

After the arrival of the Muslims in the year 711, the former Hispalis came to be known as Isbilya, the term from which its current name was derived. Until the 5th century, it competed with Cordoba for supremacy among the cities of Al-Andalus or Islamic Spain, but in the 6th century Seville imposed itself. It was the court of the Abbadid Dynasty that governed the most powerful kingdom of taifas in al-Andalus, and in the 7th and 8th centuries the Andalusian capital of the Moroccan Empire of the Almohads. From this point on and for the next four-hundred years, it would be the most important city on the Peninsula.

This was an age of brilliance, when the city was a meeting

Real Alcázar. Jardín de los Poetas.

point between East and West, and it was from this era that Seville inherited an extensive walled urban area and some of its most emblematic monuments: the **Giralda,** the **Alcázar,** and the **Torre del Oro.**

In 1248, after a long siege, the Christian army led by Ferdinand III entered this city destined to become the bastion against the final redoubt of Islam on the Peninsula. Until the fall of the Kingdom of Granada in 1492, Seville was used as a regular residence by kings such as the same Ferdinand III, his son Alfonso X the Wise – who encouraged the city's intensive cultural development – Peter I and the Catholic Monarchs. Inhabited by resettlements of Castilians and minority populations of Muslims, Jews and foreigners, at the end of the Middle Ages it was one of the most dynamic cities in the West. At the same time, the triumph of Christianity was

Cathedral. Buttresses and flying buttresses with the Giralda in the backgrownd

expressed through the building of churches, convents, and a magnificent Gothic cathedral.

Great Spanish Babylon

Seville reached its zenith between the 15th and 17th centuries thanks to its monopoly on traffic with the Indies, after the discoveries made on Columbus's journey in 1492. For decades, the fleets and galleons that by law put in at the Sevillian port, inundated the city with riches and made it one of the most booming metropolis in Europe. With a diverse and cosmopolitan population of about 150,000 inhabitants at the end of the 16th century, aristocrats and merchants rubbed shoulders in the city streets, as well as religious figures, bureaucrats, members of the military, artisans and sailors, all surrounded by a cloud of rogues and scoundrels.

Torre del Oro.

The thriving economic and mercantile activity of this "port and gate to the Indies" stimulated a brilliant artistic and cultural boom. Cervantes, Lope de Vega, Zurbarán, and a multitude of other illustrious figures coincided in Seville, and the city was the birthplace of Velázquez, Murillo and other renowned artists. This prosperity also resulted in a profound urban renovation. Plazas (squares) and avenues, such as the **Alameda de Hércules,** were laid out, and an infinite number of new buildings were erected under the sign of the Renaissance and Baroque styles.

The crisis of the Spanish crown in the middle of the 17th century marked the decline of Seville, and the devastating plague epidemic of 1649, which cut the city's population in half, symbolized the end of its golden age.

The Romantic city and the capital of Andalusia

Relegated to functioning as the regional capital of the Lower Guadalquivir in the 18th and 19th centuries, Seville's existence took on a monotonous pulse, altered only by events such as the French occupation during the War of Independence. Despite its efforts at industrialization, it remained anchored to agrarian activity and trade. Its traditional atmosphere, southern climate, and portentous artistic heritage, with exotic Arab monuments, seduced travelers, and soon forged the clichéd image of the Romantic Seville, seasoned by the myths of Don Juan, Fígaro and Carmen.

The 19th century marked the beginning of an urban transformation that accelerated into the 20th century. After the War of Independence and the confiscation (of church property), many religious buildings became private property or simply disappeared. Gates and city walls were torn down to make way for plazas and avenues, and finally, a large project was undertaken to give direction to this growth, the **Latin American Expo of 1929**. Propelled by this competition, urban expansion areas were designed and the **Santa Cruz district** and the **Parque de María Luisa** (María Luisa Park) were revamped. Modernization however, would not entirely take off until the 1960s, triggered by a moment of dramatic demographic,

Jardines de Murillo.

economic, and urban expansion. In 1982 Seville became the capital of the Autonomous Community of Andalusia, seat of its Parliament and of the regional governments, and in 1992 it became the site of another universal event – the World's Fair – which resulted in the improvement of the city's infrastructures – bridges, freeways, high-speed train – establishing the foundations for the current Seville and its extensive metropolitan area.

PATIO DE BANDERAS (FLAGS COURTYARD)

This courtyard is located in front of the Alcázar, with houses built into its wall, orange trees and a fountain in the center, making up one of the most photogenic views of Seville. It was the arms courtyard of the original 5th century Alcázar, laid over a Visigoth basilica. This patio serves as a hinge between the Alcázar and the Santa Cruz district reached by way of the narrow pasaje de la Judería (passage of the Jewish Quarter), the magical "alley of whispers" that takes off from one of its corners.

The monument district

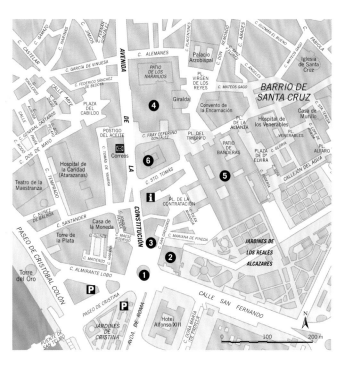

1. Puerta de Jerez
2. Palace of Yanduri
3. Chapel of Maese Rodrigo
4. Cathedral and Giralda
5. Archivo de Indias
6. Real Alcázar

Cathedral.

Seville boasts one of the most extensive old city centers in Europe. Divided by the Guadalquivir River, it has the oval shape of the city wall built by the Muslims in the 7th century. Its southern vertex is noted for the concentration of important historical buildings pertaining to the government, culture, and commerce, made up of the trio formed by the Cathedral, the Archivo de Indias (Indian Archives), and the Real Alcázar (Royal Palace), declared UNESCO World Heritage Sites in 1987.

Sevillian courtyard. Santa Cruz district.

Avenida de la Constitución

The **puerta** (gate) **de Jerez** is the entrance to the historic district. After its fortifications were torn down, it was turned into a plaza. This is the site of the **palace of Yanduri,** where there is a plaque commemorating the birthplace of the poet Vicente Aleixandre (1898-1984), winner of the 1977 Nobel Prize, and the **chapel of Maese Rodrigo,** oratory of the first Sevillian university, founded in 1506. The **avenida de la Constitución** – nicknamed la Avenida (the Avenue) – begins here, an artery of crucial importance that runs through the City Center. Opened in the early 20th century it serves as the center stage during the Semana Santa (Holy Week) and Corpus processions. The avenue is lined with beautiful regionalist style buildings, and the remains of the city

Puerta de Jerez.

Personification of Seville. The fountain in the Puerta de Jerez.

walls such as the tower of Abdelaziz and the arquillo de la Plata (arch of Silver), through which precious metals unloaded in the port were taken into the Alcázar.

The Cathedral

The cathedral buildings cover a large area halfway up la Avenida. According to traditional lore, in 1401 the Sevillian canons, vowed to make "a temple such, that those that saw it would think we were mad". A little less than a century later, in 1517, it became known as the largest Gothic church ever built, and one of the largest cathedrals in Christendom. The object of numerous reforms, it was not completely finished until the 20th century.

The Cathedral was constructed over the great 7th century mosque built by the Almohads, preserving its courtyard and tower, the Giralda. **The puerta del Perdón** (gate of Pardon), located to the north, was the principal access point. Its immense original door, bronze plated with inscriptions in Arabic, sits under the reliefs and terracotta sculptures added in the 16th century. It provides access to the **patio de los Naranjos** (Courtyard of Orange Trees), where the Muslims preformed their ritual washing before prayers. Next to it is the impressive and enormous Gothic body of the church, with a rectangular floor plan with

Cathedral and the Giralda.

Puerta del Perdón of the cathedral.

Cathedral and the patio de los Naranjos.

chapels and other side chambers. It was built by a collaboration between master stone masons from France, Spain, and Germany.

Outside, the Gothic cathedral has a vibrant display of cresting, gargoyles and pinnacles, in addition to beautiful **doorways.** The oldest of these, from the mid 15th century, are on the west side, with baked clay sculptures by Lorenzo Mercadante de Bretaña. Those to the east – doorways of los Palos and Campanillas – flaunt reliefs by Miguel Florentín. Visits begin through the rooms adjacent to the gate of San Cristóbal, oriented towards the Archivo de Indias and the Alcázar. In the admitting rooms, diverse painting – like that of *San Fernando,* by Murillo – and precious metal work hint at the artistic opulence found in this largest Sevillian church. Once inside, the astonishing magnitude of this space cannot but move

Cathedral. Puerta de la Concepción.

the visitor. It is divided into five naves with vaulting that reaches up to 36 meters in height above a forest of pillars, a grandiose atmosphere bathed in the soft light that filters through the multi-colored panes of the stained glass windows. The **Main chapel** is located in the crossing, under the golden brilliance of a majestic Gothic altar from the late 15th century, begun by the Flemish artist Pieter Dancart, and the choir, with magnificent stalls carved in the Gothic-Mudejar style and spectacular baroque organs from the 18th century. In one transcept of the cruciform, opposite a gigantic mural of San Cristóbal, lies the mausoleum of Christopher Columbus. Installed in 1898, it is overshadowed by controversy over whether or not it actually contains the remains of the Admiral. At the head of the temple is the **Capilla Real** (Royal

Cathedral. Vaulting in the crossing.

Cathedral. Naves of the choir and the organ.

Chapel), a Renaissance apse begun in 1551 and presided over by the Virgen de los Reyes – patron saint of Seville – which serves as a pantheon for the remains of San Fernando, Alfonso X the Wise, Peter I and other royalty. A sumptuous repertoire of painting, sculpture, precious metals, and other work inundates the remaining naves and chapels, among which should be noted that of San Pedro, in the head of the church, which contains a pictorial retable by Zurbarán, that of San Antonio, on the north side, which has an unusually sized painting by Murillo, the chapels of the Alabastros (Alabasters), so called for the material used in their construction, and the chapel of the Virgen de la Antigua. The largest of the chapels, it is located on the southern flank and is the home to the image of the Virgin, said to have been found by Ferdinand III on a wall of the mosque upon conquering the city.

Special attention should be given to the **sacristy of the Cálices** (Chalices), which has various tablets from the 15th and 16th centuries, as well as the oil painting of the *Santas Justa y Rufina* that Francisco de Goya painted expressly for the Cathedral in 1817, the chapel of San Andrés, across from the image of the *Cristo de la Clemencia* carved by Martínez Montañés, and, next to it, the **Main Sacristy,** a harmonious

Renaissance space planned in 1528, where the Cathedral's treasure is stored along with splendid oil paintings such as the *Descendimiento* by Pedro de Campaña, *San Isidro and San Leandro* by Murillo or *Santa Teresa de Jesús* by Zurbarán.

The richness of the chalices is surprising, along with reliquary, crosses and other jewels with liturgical silver and goldsmithing and crusted with pearls and precious stones, on display next to the masterworks of the *Custodia de Corpus* (Custody of Corpus), a 4 meter high template, and the *Tablas Alfonsíes* triptych. The areas adjacent to the temple eventually lead to the sala del Antecabildo and the **sala Capitular** (Chapterhouse), the original elliptical room designed by Hernán Ruiz el Joven in 1558 for canon meetings, covered by a painted dome by Murillo. The cathedral complex is completed with the parochial church of **Sagrario,** annexed to the patio de los Naranjos and with a separate entrance on the avenida de la Constitución. Erected in the 17th century, this baroque structure has rotundas with stone vaults and an altar by the religious artist Pedro Roldán.

SANTAS JUSTA AND RUFINA BY MURILLO
The patron saints of Seville were two pottery makers from Triana who were martyred at the beginning of the 4th century for rejecting pagan idols. They appear in an infinity of paintings, sculptures, and reliefs both in the Cathedral and other churches around the city, represented with the Giralda between them. According to legend, they appeared miraculously during an earthquake and held the tower in place to prevent its destruction.

The Giralda

The symbol of Seville, this tower rises up between the patio de los Naranjos and the Cathedral. It was commissioned by the Almohad Caliph Abu Yaqub

Cathedral and the Giralda from the patio de Banderas.

Yusuf as the minaret of the great mosque, and completed in 1198 under the direction of Ahmed Ibn Baso and Alí de Gomara. Its beautiful shaft, decorated with lengths of cut brick, is identical to the minaret of the Kutubiyya de Marrakech Mosque and the tower of Hassan de Rabat, in Morocco. Inside, the tower is climbed using a ramp designed so that a horse can reach the top. The Giralda acquired its form, magnitude and definitive name after the Christian conquest, remaining a successful example of the amalgam of cultures. In 1568 the architect Hernán Ruiz el Joven added the Renaissance bell tower, crowned by a weather vane with a 3,5 meter high bronze statue that represents the triumph of faith. The popular name for this figure – the Giraldillo, the Giralda, after its revolving movement – ended up as the name for the entire tower.

THE BEST VIEW
With its height of 95 meters, the Giralda is a privileged vantage point from which to look out over the panorama of Seville towards its four cardinal points. It is worth the climb up its ramp to contemplate, below its massive bells, the landscape of rooftops, towers, and belfries, the courtyards and enclosed gardens of palaces, convents, and houses, and many other details hidden from view to passersby.

Archivo de Indias (Indian Archives)

The most assessed example of Renaissance architecture in the Andalusian capital sits on a pedestal in front of the Alcázar. It was erected between 1583 and 1598 during the reign of Philip II under the supervision of his favorite architect, Juan de Herrera, the architect of El Escorial. Used as a Merchant's Guild, it was built to provide a meeting place for businessman. In 1785, when Charles III ordered that all of the documents relating to the overseas kingdom (the New World) be stored here, and it became the Indian Archives. Since then, it has been home to the world's most complete collection of documents relating to the history of America and the Pacific between the 15th and 19th centuries, with 90 million pages of manuscripts and 7,000 maps and drawings.

Real Alcázar

The **plaza del Triunfo** (Triumph) separates the Cathedral from the Alcázar, which is protected by the oldest walls in Seville. These were the defenses of the primitive alcázar – or fortified palace – build in 913 by Abderramán III of Cordoba. This would be the

The Giraldillo.

Archivo de Indias.

Rooms of the Archivo de Indias.

beginnings of a vast complex, adapted and altered between the 5th and 19th centuries to serve as a residence for caliphs and kings. The Real Alcázar, vastly different from other European royal palaces, better embodies the model of the Eastern citadel, where the palatine nuclei superimpose one another over time following incredibly diverse styles, which, in this case span Islamic and Mudejar art, in addition to Gothic, Renaissance, Baroque, and movements from later periods.

The **puerta del León** (gate of the Lion) is the main entrance. A few steps from here is the **sala de Justicia,** a 14th century Mudejar room looking out over the **patio del Yeso** (Plaster courtyard). Its shallow pool reflects a gallery of plaster filigrees, a suggestive reminder of the work undertaken by the Almohads, who, in the 12th and 13th centuries widened the walls, palaces, and gardens of the Alcázar turning it into an enviable oasis. From here, the **patio de la Montería** (Hunting courtyard) opens up, with the Cuarto del Almirante (Admiral's Room) off to one side. This was the location of the Casa de la Contratación (House of Contracts) where trafficking with the Indies was controlled, and in the center, lies the façade of the **palace of King Peter,** a Mudejar master-piece and the gate to the most dazzling section of the palace. Built in 1364 by Peter I it

Gardens of the Real Alcázar.

Puerta del León, Real Alcázar.

Fuente de Neptuno, Real Alcázar.

Fuente de Mercurio, Real Alcázar.

Estanque (pond) de Mercurio and galería de Grutescos, Real Alcázar.

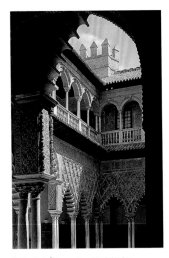

Patio de las Doncellas, Real Alcázar.

boasts sumptuous rooms decorated with tiles, plasterwork and coffering, surrounding two courtyards. That of las Muñecas (Dolls), forms the axis of the private quarters, while that of las Doncellas (Maidens), was the center of courtesan life and is connected to the palace's crown jewel, the **salón de Embajadores** (Ambassador's Room). Used as a throne room and reception hall, this large room takes advantage of an 11th century pavilion once used by the kings of Sevillian taifas, and it is sheltered by a marvelous wooden dome from the 15th century.

The upper floor contains more regal rooms in the Cuarto Real Alto (Royal High Quarters). Built in the 13th century, the somewhat more austere **Gothic palace** of Alfonso X, is where this "Wise" king composed much of his work. Some of its rooms reflect the Renaissance and Baroque styles given to them in the 16th and 18th centuries to welcome the Emperor Charles I, and King Philip V. In addition to tiles painted in the Italian style, there is a collection of Flemish tapestries that narrates the Emperor's conquest of Tunis in 1535.

Next to the palaces lies the patio del Crucero, an original garden in the shape of a cross of Almohad origin, and the pool from the baths of Mrs. María de Padilla, as well as the sensual continuation of the **gardens.** Distributed along a succession of courtyards and an area enclosed by seven hectares of walls, it makes up one of the richest and most varied examples of Spanish gardening. The Spanish-Muslim gardens that surround the palaces lead to the mannerist garden of the Estanque (Pond) and the galería de Grutescos, an elevated path running through the vegetation. This is followed by various different gardens such as that of las Damas (the Ladies), el Cenador (the Bower), with its graceful Charles I pavilion, and the Laberinto (Labyrinth) made out of myrtle hedges, until coming to the meadows of the jardín Inglés (English garden), and the Sevillian style ponds, arbors, and flowerbeds of the jardines Nuevos (New gardens). The route around the Alcázar comes to an end at the apeadero, next to the patio de Banderas.

Arch of the Peacocks, Real Alcázar.

Salón de Embajadores, Real Alcázar.

The Santa Cruz district and the City Center

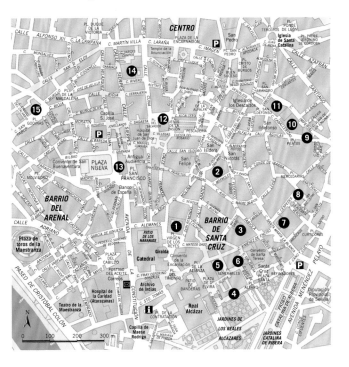

1. Archbishop's Palace
2. Temple of Hércules
3. Church of Santa Cruz
4. Callejón del Agua
5. Hospital de los Venerables
6. Murillo Home
7. Church of Santa María la Blanca
8. San Bartolomé
9. Church of San Esteban
10. Casa de Pilatos
11. Convent of San Leandro
12. Church of Divino Salvador
13. City Hall
14. Palace of Lebrija
15. Church of la Magdalena

Canvases over calle Sierpes.

The traditional and well-known Santa Cruz district is situated beneath the shadow of the Giralda and the battlements of the Alcázar. Its unmistakable aroma of whitewash and flowers and its gratifying weave of cobblestone streets and tiny plazas, drift little by little between churches and stately ancestral houses towards the City Center. Known only by this name, this is the area of the historic district where the majority of public and commercial activity has traditionally taken place.

Around the Cathedral

The streets neighboring the patio de los Naranjos – Alemanes, Hernando Colón, Álvarez Quintero, and Argote de Molina – make up a very popular area with a lively nightlife. At the foot of the Giralda is the artistic stone candelabra of the **plaza de la Virgen de los Reyes,** which lies between the reddish façade of the 17th and 18th century **Archbishop Palace** and the whitewashed walls of the 14th century convent of the Encarnación. Among the streets that make up the intricate maze surrounding the Archbishop's palace is **calle Abades,** the urban center of the Roman city, which has palaces such as the 15th–16th century casa de los Pinelo, calle Mármoles, where the columns from **Hercules' 2nd century temple** are located, and calle Guzmán el Bueno, where passageways and gates provide glimpses of deliciously wonderful courtyards.

Plaza de la Virgen de los Reyes.

Santa Cruz District

Lined with bars and shops, the permanently busy **calle Mateos Gago** leads from the Cathedral to the Santa Cruz district. At its highest point is the **church of Santa Cruz**. From the 17th and 18th centuries, it was the parish church for the area that included the Jewish Quarter. The Jewish community thrived here during the 13th and 14th centuries. and began its decline at the time of the pogroms of 1391 until the final expulsion of Spanish Jews in 1492. Rebuilt

Archibishop's Palace

Courtyard in the Santa Cruz district.

Passageway in the Jewish Quarter.

by the Tourism Board around 1920, the neighborhood exudes an old and peaceful atmosphere, sweetened by the fragrances of *azahar* (orange blossoms) from the trees that line the streets and jasmine from the courtyards.

From Mateos Gago, the streets flow along into a charming pedestrian labyrinth lined with whitewashed houses gazing out into secluded places like the plaza de la Alianza, the plaza de Doña Elvira, where there was an open-air comedy theater, and the sinuous **passageway of the calle Judería,** zigzagging its way from the patio de Banderas to the **callejón del Agua.** This narrow street follows a wall containing the pipes that supply water to the Alcázar, bordered by the house where Washington Irving – author of the Romantic *Tales from the Alhambra* – once lived, and through the narrowest of

streets with names such as Vida, Susona or Pimienta. Just a few steps away is the **Hospital de los Venerables.** Built at the end of the 17th century, it was used as a residence for elderly priests and today is the seat of a cultural foundation. Its elegant Baroque design includes a courtyard garden with paths and a church adorned with dramatic frescos by Juan de Valdés Leal and his son Lucas Valdés.

Of note in the area close to the Venerables, are the streets Mesón del Moro, which boasts the remains of an Arab bath integrated into a restaurant, and Santa Teresa, the site of the convent of San José founded by Santa Teresa de Jesús in 1576, as well as the **Murillo Home.** Around the corner from here is the **plaza de Santa Cruz,** with its orange trees surrounding the forged craftsman-

Courtyard in the Jewish Quarter.

Plaza de Santa Cruz.

Santa Cruz district.

MURILLO'S NEIGHBORHOOD

Bartolomé Esteban Murillo (1617-1682), the brilliant Baroque painter who best captured the local sensitivity, had very strong ties to the Santa Cruz district. A regular inhabitant of the area, he frequently visited the primitive parish church – whose demolition in 1810 made way for the plaza de Santa Cruz – to admire its paintings. La casa de Murillo, in the calle Santa Teresa, is one of the houses where he once lived. It is a traditional Sevillian style house built around a courtyard, with hallways, corridors and high and low rooms that were alternatively used in winter and summer.

ship of the Cruz de la Cerrajería (Cross of the Locksmiths) The statue of Don Juan Tenorio, in the immediate plaza de Refinadores, evokes the drama of his adventures and marks the limits of the Santa Cruz district, together with the **Jardines** (gardens) **de Murillo** and the **paseo** (promenade) **de Catalina de Ribera,** that carpet the strip running between the Alcázar and the calle Menéndez y Pelayo with vegetation. Laid out in the late 19th and early 20th century on what was once the Alcázar's orchards, these gardens adhere to the Sevillian model, with benches and arbors made of brick and ceramic, bowers hung with lianas – of an enormous size, and a statue of Christopher Columbus.

Santa María la Blanca and San Bartolomé

Less frequented, but equally attractive are the neighborhoods adjacent to Santa Cruz. The **church of Santa María la Blanca,** formerly a synagogue, is a distinguishing feature of

Santa Cruz district.

the neighborhood of calle San José. Its exuberant interior is covered in 17th plasterwork. It is adorned with a *Santa Cena* de Murillo. Unfortunately, the other paintings made by this artist for the church were dispersed during the War of Independence. The ins and outs of these small streets continue through San Bartolomé and the **calle Levíes,** where palaces and historic bars like la Carbonería alternate, until reaching the 14th-15th century **church of San Esteban.**

Church of San Esteban.

Gardens of the Casa de Pilatos.

Casa de Pilatos (House of Pilate)

In front of the plaza de Zurbarán is the **casa de Pilatos,** the city's most stately and important residence. It is named after the first station – Jesus before Pilate – from a Stations of the Cross that was begun at the palace gates. A rare combination of materials and styles are evidence of the artistic mixture that was forged in Seville at the beginning of the Modern Age. The impetus for this construction was Don Fadrique Enríquez de Ribera, model sponsor of the Renaissance Movement, upon his return from the Holy Land in 1519. Through the classic Genoan door and the *apeadero* lies the principal courtyard, with its Carrara marbles, Greek and Roman statues, Renaissance busts, Gothic plasterwork, and Mudejar ceramics, refinements that also charac-

terize the rooms and gardens of the lower floor – the chapel, the salón del Pretorio, the Zaquizami corridor, the Chico (Small) and Grande (Large) gardens, Pilate's office... –. A grandiose staircase covered in painted tiles and a wooden dome leads to the rooms on the upper floor known for their first rate paintings, murals and painted ceilings like the one by Francisco Pacheco, the mentor and father-in-law of Velázquez. The **convent of San Leandro** (14th – 17th centuries) is located on the same block as the casa de Pilatos facing the church of San Ildefonso. It is known for the sweets prepared and sold here by the nuns.

El Salvador and la Encarnación

The unhurried rhythm of traditional Seville can be savored on the walk towards the **plaza del Salvador,** one of the coziest places in the Center, and an ideal spot to have a drink in front of its Baroque church and the hospital de la Paz. The origins of the city can be felt in the ancient and authentic air of these streets, some of which, a rarity in Seville, are slightly inclined. Calles Francos and Álvarez Quintero, the **plaza del Pan** (behind Salvador), and the calle Alcaicería are the redoubt of small business, while the church of San Isidoro (14th - 18th centuries and the **plaza de la Alfalfa** represent the religious and social poles of the highest

Main courtyard, Casa de Pilatos.

Sculptures and galleries in the main courtyard, Casa de Pilatos.

Plaza del Salvador.

place in the Center. A labyrinth of small streets connects la Alfalfa with the plazas de **la Encarnación,** and Cristo de Burgos, in front of the **church of San Pedro** (14th-18th centuries). Joined by calle Imagen, they now neighbor the more working class neighborhoods.

Plaza de San Francisco and Plaza Nueva

City Hall and the plazas de San Francisco and Nueva at the end of the avenida de la Constitución, mark the neurological focus of the City Center or Centro, the name for the historic area that brings together the principal shopping districts. The **plaza de San Francisco,** flanked by houses with balconies, has been host to a public forum once used for markets, autos-da-fé, and bull events; and today the boxes and altars for the processions are assembled here. Its name comes

> **CHURCH OF THE DIVINO SALVADOR**
> The second most important church in Seville after the Cathedral is also the one with the longest history. Built over a Roman temple and a Visigoth basilica, this was also once the location of the first High Mosque in Seville, substituted in the 17th and 18th centuries by this great Baroque building. The original courtyard from the 9th century mosque is preserved next to it, as is the foot of the minaret, turned into a bell tower.

from the Franciscan convent that occupied the nearby lot, demolished in 1867 to make way for the **Plaza Nueva,** the largest square in the Center, presided over by an equestrian statue of San Fernando. The **City Hall** is located between these two plazas, whose two façades reflect their different characters. San Francisco has a multi-colored

Church of Divino Salvador.

High Altar of Salvador.

THE SYMBOL OF SEVILLE

On the reliefs adorning the plateresque façade of City Hall there is a curious symbol – NO8DO – which is repeated all over the city. It is a hieroglyph linking the syllables NO and DO with a stylized version of a skein, known as a madeja. It should be read "no madeja do", "no me ha dejado" which means approximately "you didn't leave me". According to tradition, this emblem was bestowed on Seville at the end of the 13th century by Alfonso X the Wise, as a reward for its loyalty during the dynastic conflicts that were on the verge of removing him from power.

Plaza Nueva. Monument to San Fernando.

panel of 16th century plateresque reliefs, while the 19th century façade of the plaza Nueva demonstrates its Neoclassical order.

Calle Sierpes

Pedestrian by definition, narrow, irregular, varied and boisterous, **calle Sierpes** provides the best condensed version of life in its many forms. During the hot summer months it takes on a very Sevillian tone when canvases are stretched over the streets to shade them from the sun. Between the casino windows and store fronts decorated with Spanish shawls and fans, near jewelry stores and other kinds of shops, this street's journey from plaza de San Francisco to La Campana marks the axis of Seville's City Center. The bustle carries over to the side streets, peppered with bars, cafes, and other sights like the tiny chapel of San José, with its surprising and exultant Baroque interior. Running parallel to calle Sierpes on one side is **calle Tetuán,** replete with modern shops, and on the other side **calle Cuna,** more traditional, with the noble entrance to the **palace of Lebrija** at number eight. Calle Sierpes then makes its way to plaza de **La Campana** and its popular patisserie, a crossroads where the activity continues. This same hustle and bustle can be found in the **plaza del Duque** just across the street, where a statue of Velázquez erected in 1892, sits on its pedestal above the square.

City Hall. Plaza de San Francisco.

Plaza de San Francisco.

Church of la Magdalena.

The Magdalena

From calle Sierpes towards the river there is another very busy area surrounding the calles Méndez Núñez, Rioja and O'Donnell, and converging in the **plaza de la Magdalena.** The church of this same name (13th-17th centuries) merits notice both for its elaborate Baroque architecture, and its history. It was part of the Dominican convent of San Pablo where the first court of the Spanish Inquisition was established in 1480, and inside there is a mural depicting an auto-da-fé. The church's exceptional collection of artwork includes painting by Zurbarán, frescos, and statues by the finest religious icon makers of the 17th century. From the Magdalena, **calle Reyes Católicos** leads away from the Center and widens in the direction of the paseo de Colón.

DIEGO VELÁZQUEZ

This world renowned painter was born in 1599 in the Sevillian neighborhood known as la Morería (the Moorish Quarter), on the calle de la Gorgoja, now calle Padre Luis María Llop, next to the plaza del Cristo de Burgos. He was baptized in the church of San Pedro, in the same baptismal that is there today. He spent his first years in Seville and in 1623 moved to Madrid in the service of Philip IV, establishing himself in the Court until his death in 1660.

Calle Sierpes.

Calle Sierpes. Círculo de Labradores (Worker's Guild).

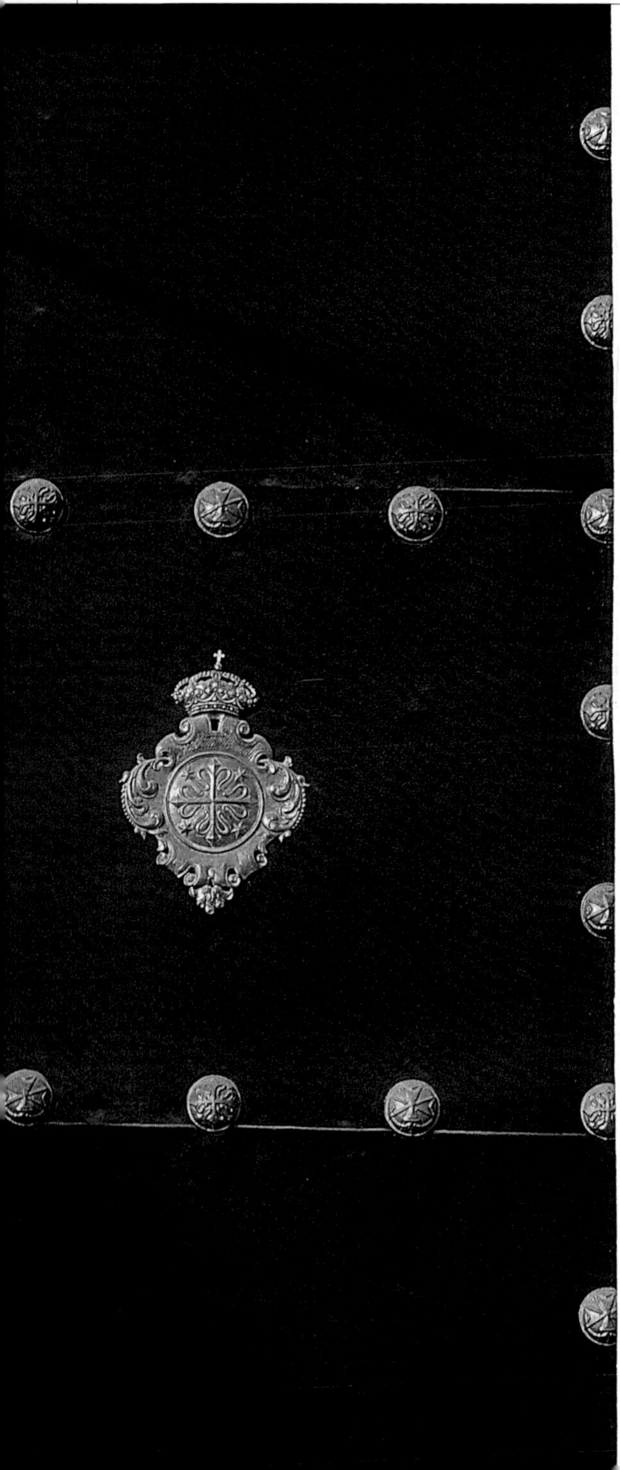

The Museum and the neighborhoods

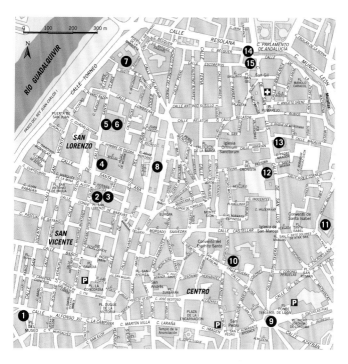

1. Museum of Fine Arts
2. San Lorenzo parish
3. Basilica of the Gran Poder
4. Convent of Santa Ana
5. Torre de Don Fadrique
6. Convent of Santa Clara
7. Convent of San Clemente
8. Alameda de Hércules
9. Church of Santa Catalina
10. Palace of las Dueñas
11. Monastery of Santa Paula
12. Church of San Luis
13. Church of Santa Marina
14. Arco de la Macarena
15. Basilica of the Macarena

Door of the church of Omnium Sanctorum (detail).

Located in the vicinity of the City Center, the Museum of Fine Arts (Museo de Bellas Artes) is an essential stop during a visit to Seville. Also of great interest are the residential neighborhoods (detailed below) that occupy the majority of the historic City Center. With their parishes, plazas and markets, each one forms its own microcosm in the city's interior. Within this compact urban framework, la Alameda de Hércules, divides the well-to-do neighborhoods that extend to the west towards calle Torneo and the river, from the working class neighborhoods located to the east and the north towards the Macarena.

Museum of Fine Arts

Just a few steps away from plaza del Duque and the Magdalena is the tranquil plaza that lies in front of the museum, with its statue of Murillo and large trees. Located in the old convent of the Merced Calzada, founded in the 8th century and rebuilt at the beginning of the 17th century, it was finally converted into a museum in the 19th century. A dignified seat for the second most important art gallery in Spain, housing exceptional collections of paintings and sculptures from the Middle Ages to the 20th century, including the most complete series from the Seville Baroque School, and permanent collections that include ceramics, furniture, architecture and decorative arts. The physiognomy of the building

follows the general lines set out by the ambitious renovation of the medieval building in 1602 by the architect Juan de Oviedo, who created an example of mannerist aesthetics organized around various courtyards, with a monumental staircase and a voluminous church. The vestibule is decorated in brightly colored figurative tile (called *azulejos*) and leads to the patio del Aljibe, also with decorated panels and baseboards, the patio de la Conchas, and the garden-courtyard patio de los Bojes.

Monument to Murillo and façade of the Museum of Fine Arts

These **courtyards** serve as entrances to the first rooms containing art from the end of the Middle Ages, with gilded panels in styles falling between Gothic, Flemish and the early Renaissance, together with notable sculptures such as the terracotta *Virgen con el Niño* by Lorenzo Mercadante de Bretaña. Following the museum's chronological and stylistic organization, next is a selection of art from the 16th century that reflects the formation of the Sevillian Pictorial School and other pieces from

Museum of Fine Arts. Sala de la Iglesia.

Zurbarán. *San Hugo en el refectorio (detail).*

artists of varying backgrounds, such as the *Stations of the Cross* by Lucas Cranach, the striking statue of *San Jerónimo* made of polychrome baked clay and sculpted in 1525 by the peer and rival of Miguel Ángel Pietro Torrigiano, and the portrait of *Jorge Manuel Theotocopoulos,* painted by his father, El Greco, in 1600.

The appearance of Sevillian art between the 16th and 17th century, can be contemplated in various carvings depicting religious imagery and oil paintings done by artists such as Juan de las Roelas or Francisco Pacheco, whose workshop was the starting place for the young Velázquez. The prosperity of this local school is captured in the **spaciousness of the church,** an atmosphere rife with generous proportions and vaulted ceilings decorated with murals made up of squares that come together in the large formats

of Zurbarán, Murillo, and other masters. Francisco de Zurbarán, who came to Seville from the province of Extremadura, produced the figures of saintly monks, and in 1631 his most important piece, the *Apoteosis de Santo Tomás de Aquino.* The mastery of Murillo dazzles at the head of the church, where there is a *Blessed Virgin,* known as *La Colosal* (The Colossal) for its magnitude, the *Santas Justa and Rufina, Santo Tomás de Villanueva, Our Lady of Sorrows,* and other displays of his fluent brush strokes and soft colors, a style that is condensed in the intimate expressiveness of the small *Virgin de la servilleta.*

The **large cloister** and **imperial staircase** covered in plasterwork, lead to the upper rooms where the renewal of the Sevillian Baroque style continues, together with the work of other Spanish, Flemish, and Italian painters from the 17th century. Zurbarán's series on the Cartuja – representative of his perfectionism with regards to lines and colors – is on display, as are diverse sacred figures by José de Ribera, oil paintings of saints where the precise naturalism of vehement chiaroscuros can be appreciated, and work by the Sevillian Juan de Valdés Leal, whose depictions of San Jerónimo and other canvases demonstrate his energetic dramatism. Students of Murillo and Hispalese painting from the 18th century are the focus of the contiguous spaces in this museum, whose founding was nurtured by the abundance of artistic heritage coming from the dozens of convents and religious foundations that were dismantled in the first half of the 19th century as a result of the War of Independence and the laws of the liberal governments.

Murillo. *La Immaculada* called *La Colosal.*

Two small Goya paintings and the galleries containing portraits and historical paintings from the Romantic period make up the final wing of the museum, which also includes traditional paintings from the last Sevillian school, such as the popular oil painting called *Las Cigarreras* by Gonzalo Bilbao.

Gonzalo Bilbao. *Las Cigarreras.*

San Lorenzo

The calle **San Vicente,** which ends at the square in front of the Museum, and the **plaza de San Lorenzo** are the reference points for the bourgeois neighborhoods, and there is length of long streets scattered with convents. The San Lorenzo parish is of Mudejar origin, built over a mosque and reformed successively until the 18th century. Next to it is the **basilica of the Gran Poder,** the sanctuary of Nuestro Padre Jesús del Gran Poder, a masterpiece carved in 1620 by Juan de Mesa, and the most solemn of the Semana Santa (Holy Week) processions. The area around the tranquil plaza de San Lorenzo is good for having tapas, and this plaza is the confluence of the calles Conde De Barajas, where the Romantic poet Gustavo Adolfo Béquer was born at number 28, and Santa Clara, marked by the

Convent of San Clemente.

cloisters of Santa Ana. Santa Clara is also known for the 13th century torre de Don Fadrique (tower) in an interior garden, and **San Clemente,** a peaceful haven founded by San Fernando under cypress and orange trees.

Alameda de Hércules

Laid out in 1574 over a lagoon formed by the river's flooding, the rectangular form of this tree-lined avenue is a relief from the close-ness of the town. At its head, there are two Roman columns from calle Mármoles with statues of Hercules and Caesar, the mythical founders of Hispalis. The Alameda has gone through many ups and downs, from being the city's most distinguished promenade, to serving as a leisure area for the working class, and later an area of ill repute. Some years ago its reputation was recovered thanks to efforts at

San Lorenzo parish

Alameda de Hércules.

"El Jueves" street market in calle Feria.

urban renewal and the proliferation of cafes and other establishments that have converted it into an area with a certain bohemian and juvenile flare.

Calle Feria and San Luis

The city's more modest nerve is on the calles Feria and San Luis, which run through the city from the Center to the Macarena. On its outskirts is the magnificent Mudejar and Baroque **church of Santa Catalina** (14th-18th centuries) and a handful of narrow streets that weave between convents and noble houses such as the **Palace of the Dueñas,** belonging to the Duke and Duchess of Alba. One of these homes was

CONVENT OF SANTA PAULA
This convent of cloistered Geronimo nuns founded in 1475, is especially known for its vestibule, its church (which has a magnificent brick and ceramic door) and its museum containing paintings, precious metals and other pieces of sacred artwork. The nuns are renowned for their jams and traditional sweets.

El Rinconcillo. Bar.

EL RINCONCILLO

Tucked into a corner of the calle Gerona in front of the church of Santa Catalina, this tavern is said to be the oldest in Seville, founded in 1670. The quality of its traditional décor – glass cases, painted tiles, and a wooden bar – and of its drinks and tapas – cured ham, *pavías* spinach with garbanzos – are equaled to its vitality as a popular place for gatherings.

the birthplace, in 1875, of the poet Antonio Machado, who wrote "My infancy is memories of a courtyard in Seville / a bright garden where the lemon tree grows…" From the parish of San Juan de la Palma, the **calle Feria** winds along until it reaches the ancient 13th-14th century church of Omnium Sanctorum and the market which crackles with the ingenuity of the neighborhood's inhabitants, as does the street market held every Thursday.

Further enmeshed, **calle San Luis,** which used to be calle Real, snakes along at the same pace, always going north, away from the Mudejar church of San Marcos. In its outlaying areas lies the outstanding **Convent of Santa Paula** (15th-17th centuries). A visit to this convent provides an unique opportunity to become enraptured in the peaceful atmosphere and the overwhelming artistic heritage found in its cloisters, not to mention a taste of its handmade pastries. Further down is the 18th century **church of San Luis,** which boasts the most daring and dynamic Baroque composition in all of Seville, with spiraling columns ascending towards the fantasy of light and color in the airy dome. The old church of Santa Marina, with its mosque-like appearance, and the plaza del Pumarejo, accompany the street on its descent towards the arco de la Macarena (arch of the Macarena).

Church of San Luis.

Dome and lantern in the church of San Luis.

PARLIAMENT OF ANDALUSIA

Across from the entrance to the Macarena is the large façade of the parliament of the Autonomous Community of Andalusia. This Renaissance style building, built starting in 1546, was once the old hospital de la Sangre or de las Cinco Llagas. Considered a masterpiece of masonry art, its church, which includes an assembly room, was designed in 1558 by Hernán Ruiz el Joven, the architect who designed the top of the Giralda's belfry.

The Macarena

Located at the opposite end of the historic district with respect to the area of the Cathedral, the Macarena has a very distinct, and much more traditional personality. The most characteristic features of this neighborhood are its **walls,** laid out by the Almoravids and Almohads at the beginning of the 9th century. They are made up of a double defensive line with towers, shutters and, in their extreme the **arco de la Macarena,** which owes its current Baroque appearance to a refurbishment at the beginning of the 19th century. As important, and for many people even more important than these walls, is the **basilica of the Macarena,** built in 1949 to house the Virgen de la Esperanza (Hope) – or Esperanza Macarena – the most fervently revered and traditionally loved Semana Santa procession.

Arco de la Macarena (detail).

Torre de Don Fadrique.

Virgen de la Macarena.

The Guadalquivir, Triana and the Cartuja

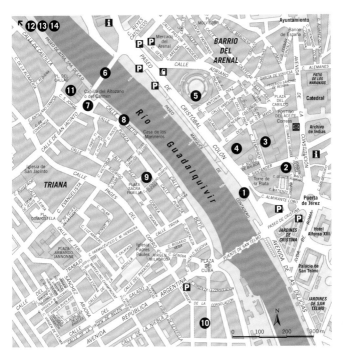

1. Paseo de Colón
2. Casa de la Moneda
3. Hospital de la Caridad (Atarazanas)
4. Teatro de la Maestranza
5. Plaza de toros de la Maestranza
6. Puente de Triana
7. Plaza del Altozano
8. Calle Betis
9. Church of Santa Ana
10. District Los Remedios
11. The Market
12. Puente del Alamillo
13. The Cartuja
14. The Olympic Stadium

Puente de Triana.

Seville opens up along the wide view drawn by the lazy course of the Guadalquivir River. Facing the narrowness of the historic district, this area is dominated by grand avenues and promenades. A route where the two river banks of Seville and Triana face each other. The city's two faces defined by the artery of the river.

The paseo de Colón and the Arenal

The **paseo de Colón** is the riverfront of the historic district of Seville, the length that runs along the riverbank between the torre del Oro (Golden Tower) and the puente de Triana (Triana Bridge). This was once the location of the port until it was shifted further downriver to its current location next to the V Centenario bridge and the SE-30 ring road. For centuries this area was a simple arenal, or sandy area, exposed to flooding and inhabited by humble settlements. Upon development it was given the name **the Arenal,** and it is currently one of the liveliest districts thanks to the presence of the bullring, the Maestranza Theater, and the many tapas bars. The gardens of the paseo Marqués de Contadero run along the paseo de Colón in front of the moorings from the boats that offer river tours and colorful views of the other bank, the Triana district.

Guadalquivir River and the Torre del Oro.

The paseo de Colón.

Torre del Oro

This Sevillian symbol is reflected in the river, called the Betis by the Romans, and the "great river", ued el-kebir, by the Arabs. A polygonal tower, it was built by the Almohads in 1220 to keep watch over the access to the port. Its name is one of the city's great mysteries. Some attribute it to the golden tone that it takes on at dusk, or to its former purpose of guarding the king's treasures and the galleons that arrived from America. The tower marks the final extreme of the walls that

MARITIME MUSEUM

Inside the torre del Oro there is a small museum that boasts a collection of maritime curiosities and different aspects of Seville's naval history and river navigation. One of its exhibitions summarizes the around the world journey completed by Juan Sebastián Elcano, who departed from the port of Seville in 1519 and returned to the torre del Oro in 1522; while another displays the designs for the Betis, Spain's first steamship, built in the Triana shipyards and launched in these waters in 1817.

connected the port to the Alcázar. The next link in this chain was the **torre de la Plata** (Silver Tower) located in the calle Santander surrounded by the alleyways of the old **Casa de la Moneda** (Mint), where the cargos of silver and gold brought from the Indies were converted into coins.

Hospital de la Caridad

In front of the torre de la Plata is the line of medieval **shipyards,** a series of large parallel warehouses from the port's dockyard. The hospital de la Caridad, a Baroque jewel, was built in the 17th century out of part of these, promoted by Miguel de Mañara who is said to have been the inspiration for the character Don Juan. It consists of two courtyards with Italian marble fountains and a church with ceramic paintings on the façade. The writing on the church's threshold reads "here lie

Church of the hospital de la Caridad.

the bones...of the worst man that the world has ever known"..., the epitaph of Mañara's tomb which serves as the culmination of the discussion about the fleetingness of life that he himself dictated to the best artists of the time. In fact, inside, the temple contains moving canvases depicting scenes of death and vanity painted by Juan

Teatro de la Maestranza.

de Valdés Leal in 1672, and a series of oil painting from Murillo's later years, the most outstanding being those of *Santa Isabel de Hungría* and *San Juan de Dios.* Next to the Caridad, behind the **teatro** (theater) **de la Maestranza,** there are various warehouses from the Atarazanas that have conserved their original appearance based on large arches and open spaces, today used for art expositions.

Plaza de toros de la Maestranza

From the Shipyards and the **postigo del Aceite** – one of the gates of the city wall – the streets of Arenal lead between bars and a number of Flamenco clubs known as "tablao", to the **plaza de toros de la Maestranza** (Maestranza bullring), located on the paseo de Colón. Its name comes from its holding institution the Real Maestranza de Caballería (the

BULLFIGHTING MUSEUM
Dedicated to the origins of the Real Maestranza de Caballería, and the history and art of bullfighting in Seville, this museum contains paintings, drawings, posters, and documents; sculptures, bullfighting costumes; and a large and diverse collection including a cape signed by Picasso.

Royal Arsenal Cavalry), a noble corporation established in the 17th century to promote the military training of the nobility. An authentic "cathedral" of bullfighting which has witnessed many of the most significant bullfighters and kills in the history of bullfighting, it was one of the first circular bullrings made with hewn stone, begun in 1761 and finished over a century later. It is also one of the most beautiful, due to its puerta del Príncipe (gate of the Prince) – only opened for those who triumph – its carved stone box, and the harmonious relationship between the floor of the bullring – with its characteristic ocher-yellow color – and the stands crowned with arcades. The plaza is completed by the pens, stables, bullfighter's chapel and the Museo Taruino (Bullfighting Museum).

Plaza de toros de la Maestranza.

CALLE BETIS

The façade of Triana, this riverside street is one of the most beautiful in the city with excellent views of the panorama of Seville including the Giralda and the Cathedral, the bullfighting ring, the torre del Oro and the Guadalquivir River. The perfect place to relax in one of the street's many sidewalk bars, kiosks, and terraces, and to try some tapas or the typical dish of pescaíto frito (fried fish).

Puente de Triana.

The puente de Triana and the Altozano

The neighborhood known as Triana is located on the right bank of the Guadalquivir River, across from Seville. It is only natural to differentiate between the banks of Seville and Triana, with their distinctly different per-sonalities. The river can be crossed at the **puente (bridge) de Isabel II,** also known as "the iron", or at the puente Triana. Inaugurated in 1852, this was the city's first permanent bridge on a river that was previously only crossed by boat. It leads to the **plaza del Altozano,** the junction where the district's principal streets meet. Next to the bridge are the small chapel nicknamed "el mechero" (the lamp) and the Market, erected on the foundations of the castle of San Jorge where the offices of the Inquisition were located. Its cellar still contains traces of these sinister courtyards and rooms in which thousands of people were condemned.

Triana District

The streets of this ancient district of sailors, potters, and wayfarers stretch out on either side of the Altozano. Famed for being lively and high-spirited, this area is also considered the hotbed of Flamenco artists and bullfighters. If the **calle Betis** opens up along the river embankment where the boats are moored, the calle Pureza – which is nothing like its name (purity) – is its interior artery. The chapel of the Marineros (sailors) is home to the Virgen de la Esperanza, mistress of the devo-

Triana district. Ceramics shop.

Puente del Alamillo (Alamillo bridge).

tion of the people of Triana during Holy Week. Around the corner from Pureza is the tiny **plaza Santa Ana,** with its 13-18th century church that serves as the neighborhood's cathedral, an example of early Gothic style seldom found in these parts. The modern area known as **los Remedios,** is animated by intense commercial activity around calle Asunción and avenida República Argentina. At the end of the puente de San Telmo, in the plaza de Cuba, lies the ancient Franciscan convent of Los Remedios that the area is named for, currently housing the Carriage Museum.

Triana spreads out along the calle San Jacinto and the **calle Castilla,** along the riverfront above the Altozano and the Market. The quadrant defined by these two streets guards many delights. The area abounds with workshops specializing in the famous Triana pottery, bars serving delicious tapas, and flower filled courtyards – such as the one in calle Castilla, 16 – in addition to places where you can listen to authentic "cante hondo" or traditional Flamenco singing, in addition to the chapels of Nuestra Señora de la O (17th and 18th century) and of the Patrocinio, sanctuary of the Cristo de la Expiración known as "el Cachorro", a Baroque image of vigorous pathos.

ALAMILLO BRIDGE

The most striking of the six new bridges that were built over the Guadalquivir for the 1992 World's Fair, it was designed by the architect and engineer Santiago Calatrava. With a monumental 138 meter pylon – the city's first structure to rise higher than the Giralda –and hanging cables that hold the 200 meter long platform, it quickly became the symbol of contemporary Seville.

Monastery of the Cartuja.

The Cartuja

Upriver from Triana is the Cartuja, site of **the 1992 World's Fair,** that is used today for administrative, business, and recreational purposes. In the midst of these modern buildings is the historic group of **monuments known as the Cartuja,** seat of the Andalusian Center of Contemporary Art. Established around 1399, this ancient monastery of Cartujo monks was once one of the richest. After the monks abandoned it in the 19th century, it was converted into a china factory. Its most outstanding features are the church, the chapel where the remains of Christopher Columbus were temporarily kept, the Mudejar cloister and a room containing very fine Renaissance sepulchers imported from Geneva.

Other buildings that stand out along the length of The Cartuja are the Navigation Pavilion, the massive Torre Triana, the Isla Mágica theme park and the Barqueta and Alamillo bridges. The surrounding areas include the **Olympic Stadium**, inaugurated in 1999, with 72,000 seats, and the park of the Alamillo, next to the bridge of the same name. With approximately 100 hectares it has two lakes and small forests with native trees and shrubs.

Ovens from the ceramics factory of the Cartuja.

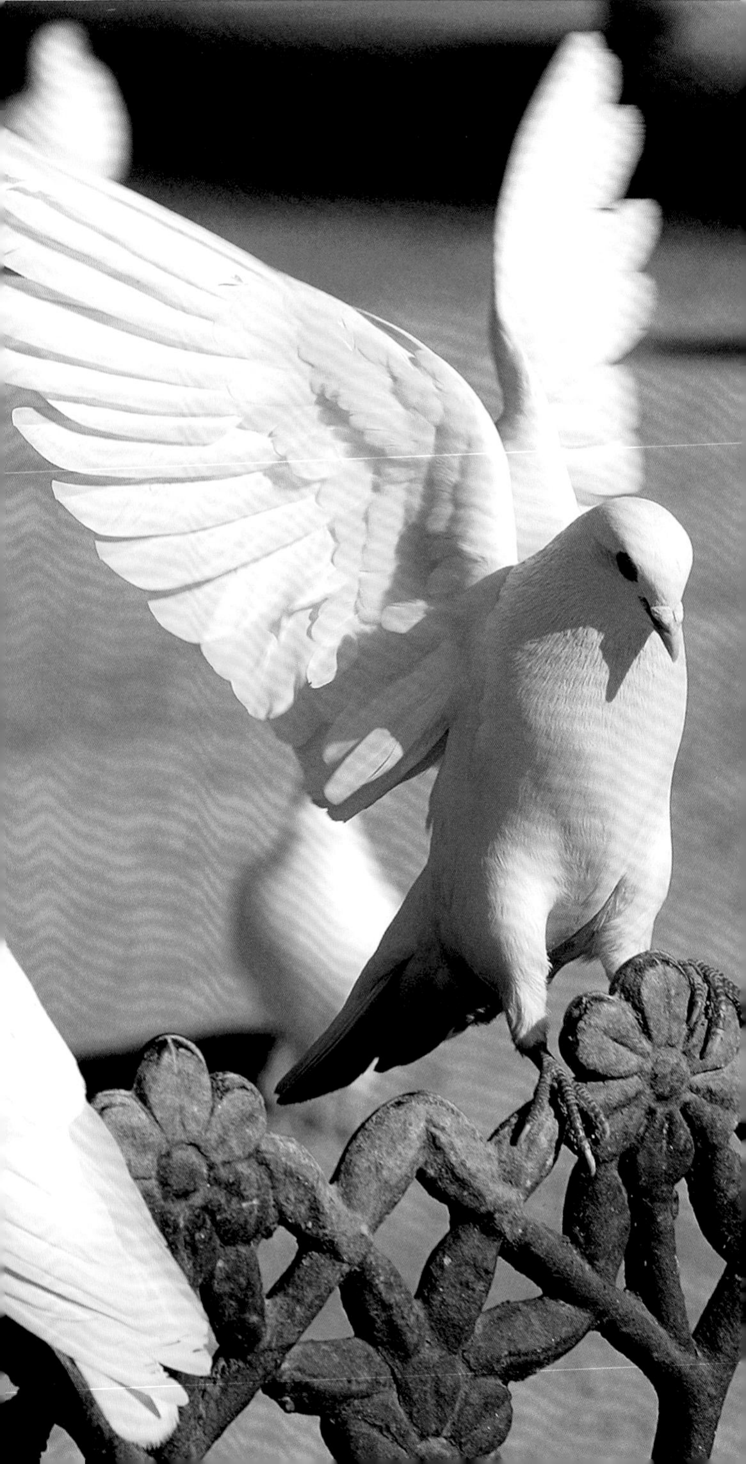

Parque de María Luisa

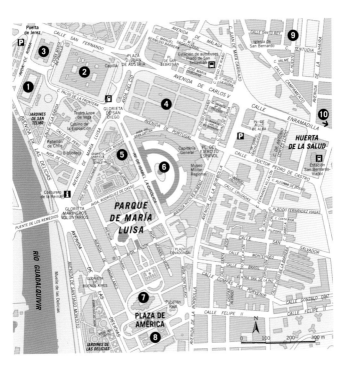

1. Palace of San Telmo
2. Real Fábrica de Tabacos
3. Hotel Alfonso XIII
4. Parque de María Luisa
   Prado de San Sebastián
5. Parque de María Luisa
   Glorieta de Bécquer
6. Plaza de España
7. Plaza de América
   Museum of Arts and Local Customs
8. Plaza de América
   Archeological Museum
9. San Bernardo district
10. Nervión district

Plaza de América.

Antigua Real Fábrica de Tabacos (Royal Tobacco Factory)

The growth outside the city walls that surrounded the historic center of Seville mostly dates to the beginning of the 20th century. Until then, the area outside the walls mainly consisted of a few humble settlements and isolated buildings. The celebration of the Latin American Expo of 1929 here, sparked the urban expansion towards the south and surrounding the axis laid out by the Parque de María Luisa (María Luisa Park), while it stimulated expansion towards the east through the Nervión neighborhood that today marks one of the central points of the modern city.

Palace of San Telmo and Real Fábrica de Tabacos (Royal Tobacco Factory)

The **palace of San Telmo,** between the puerta de Jerez and the river, was begun in 1682 for the University of Mareantes, a nautical school for pilots in the Race

UNIVERSAL MYTHS

Seville is the setting of two of the most important myths about romantic love. The ruthless figure of Don Juan was given form in 17th century theater based on the gentlemen of fortune that, respecting neither homes nor convents, swarmed in Seville during its Golden Age. The figure of Carmen, the romantic heroine of liberty and fatal passion, was inspired by the workers from the Real Fábrica de Tabacos. Created by the writer P. Mérimée, it reached world renown thanks to the opera by G.Bizet that premiered in 1875.

to the Indies. It was distinguished by the color of its façade, the towers in its corners and the sumptuous Baroque door added in 1735. In 1849 it was the home to the tiny court of the Dukes of Montpensier, from the French Orleans dynasty, who turned it into a center for political intrigues and cultural events.

Hotel Alfonso XIII. Chair and table where King Alfonso XIII worked.

It is currently the seat of the Presidency of the Government of Andalusia. Next to San Telmo, the colossal rectangular stone building – 185 by 147 meters – of the old **Real Fábrica de Tabacos,** is today a part of the university. This enormous establishment of the tobacco monopoly was built in the middle of the 18th century. With a moat, offices, chapel, its own jail, and large manufacturing spaces, it constituted its own citadel where approximately five thousand people, mostly women, worked during the 19th century. The Hotel **Alfonso XIII** is located directly next to the old factory. It only takes a walk around the courtyard of this seductive place, built in 1928, to absorb its regional style combined with a touch of colonialism.

The Park

The distribution of the land behind the Real Fábrica de Tabacos is a result of the 1929 Expo. It is an area of large green spaces with pavilions and monuments erected in honor of the event. The glorieta del Cid (roundabout) – known as "el caballo" or "the horse" after the large equestrian statue of el Cid – serves as the entrance to the gar-

Balcony of the palace of San Telmo.

Parque de María Luisa. Avenue of Hernán Cortés.

GLORIETA DE BÉCQUER

This circular monument dedicated to the Sevillian poet Gustavo Adolfo Bécquer, is one of the most suggestive in the park. It consists of a sculpture made in 1911 by L. Coullaut Valera, featuring a bust of the artist and the personifications of love in three of its stages – hoped for, fully conceived, and lost – around a lovely taxodio or bald cypress tree planted in 1850.

dens of **Prado de San Sebastián,** the original site of the Feria de Abril was first founded, and the **parque de María Luisa,** the city's finest park. It was created from the gardens of the palace of San Telmo, donated to the city in 1893 by the Princess María Luisa de Borbón, for whom it was named. With over 38 hectares, it boasts a large variety of vegetation including over 3,500 trees and almost 1,000 palm trees. At the beginning of the 20th century it was renovated by J.C. Nicolas Forestier, a park conservationist from Paris who gave the park both an Andalusian and Sevillian tone by combining Hispanic-Muslim, Romantic, and Regional influences. The 1929 Expo enriched it with diverse buildings giving the park an original feel full of variety and charm. Highlights are the brick roundabouts and painted tiles dedicated to artists and writ-

Parque de María Luisa.

ers, as well as the ceramic fountains, picturesque touches such as the Moorish Costurero de la Reina, and the central avenue that runs from the estanque de los Lotos (Lotus pond) and the isleta de los Patos (Duck island), with its exotic oriental temple, to the jets of water in the jardín de los Leones (garden of the Lions) and the cascada del Monte Gurugú, (Mount Gurugú waterfall)

Plaza de España and plaza de América

The park's boulevards lead to the gigantic **plaza de España,** symbol and legacy of the Latin American Expo of 1929. It was designed by Aníbal González, an architect inspired by regionalism – the trend that promoted the recovery of the historic styles and traditional techniques used in the construction of Seville – and fin-ished in 1928. Made of reddish brick with two 80 meter high towers united by a gallery of arches, a series of ceramic retables dedicated to the Spanish provinces and a small river, it is without a doubt one of Seville's most representative monuments. The paths between the vegetation lead to the **plaza de América,** the

Plaza de España.

Plaza de España.

Pabellón Real.

other main area of the park. The **pabellón Mudéjar,** built in 1914, is located on one side, across from it is the **Museum of Arts and Local Customs,** and the **Archeological Museum** is at the far end. Its collection brings together a large number of valuable pieces from Prehistoric Times and the Early Middle Ages, mostly from Seville, its surrounding areas, and Western Andalusia. Highlights are the Neolithic finds, bell-shaped pottery, jewels from the Tartessian civilization. and especially the collection of

The Pabellón Mudéjar, houses the Museum of Arts and Local Customs.

MUSEUM OF ARTS AND LOCAL CUSTOMS
The beautiful Moorish architecture of the Mudejar pavilion frames these ethnographic collections from Seville and Western Andalusia. Its pieces include ceramics, furniture, wood and metal work, textiles, household utensils, and farming tools, as well as other objects of anthropological interest.

Roman pieces that includes mosaics, bronzes, glass, coins, ceramics, sepulchers, and statues. The marvelous collection of Roman sculptures from the ruins of Itálica include first rate pieces like *Venus, Mercury,* and other gods, and the effigies and portraits of *Alexander the Great, Trajan* and *Hadrian.* Between the pavilions of the plaza de América is the tiny plaza de las Palomas, where children love to feed the hoards of pigeons. From the park, the avenida de la Palmera takes off in the direction of Cadiz.

From San Bernardo to Nervión

To the east of the park, the Prado and the Santa Cruz district, and through the puerta de la Carne, is the more modest **San Bernardo** area, nicknamed the "bullfighter's neighborhood" for the numerous famous matadors born here. Next to it are the gardens of the Buhaira, planted over a garden laid out by the Almohad caliphs in the 7th century, known as al-Buhayra, or "la laguna" (the lagoon) These gardens include a Neo-Moorish pavilion, a pond, and the irrigation channels of the medieval area, as well as the groves of ancient orchards, ornamental shrubs, and aromatic plants. Past Buhaira, the avenida de Eduardo Dato leads to the city's modern nucleus consolidated in the neighborhood **Nervión,** with various shopping centers offering stores, cinemas, restaurants, and other establishments that have made this area one of the most popular areas in the city today.

Excursions around the province

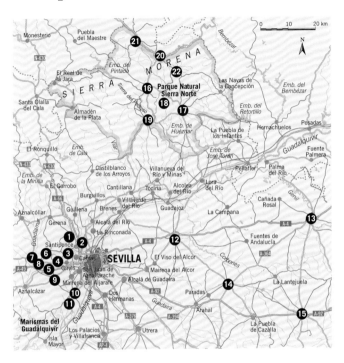

1. Itálica
2. Monastery of San Isidoro del Campo
3. Valencina de la Concepción
4. Espartinas
5. Umbrete
6. Olivares
7. Sanlúcar la Mayor
8. Hacienda Benazuza
9. Bollullos
10. Coria del Río
11. Puebla del Río
12. Carmona
13. Écija
14. Marchena
15. Osuna
16. Cazalla de la Sierra
17. Constantina
18. Sierra Norte Natural Park
19. El Pedroso
20. Alanís
21. Guadalcanal
22. San Nicolás del Puerto

Itálica. Mosaic in the casa del Planetario.

Itálica, the Aljarafe and the Marismas

The area immediately to the west of Seville offers a variety of different sites and varying landscapes that are attractive destinations for an excursion: the Roman ruins of Itálica, the hills of the Aljarafe and the immense horizon of the Marismas (the wetlands) of the Guadalquivir River.

One of the most important Roman sites on the Peninsula is located just 7km from Seville on the A-66 highway. The city of **Itálica** was founded in the year 206 BC by Scipio Africanus. An aristocratic city from the beginning, it was the birthplace of the great Roman emperors Trajan and Hadrian, whose splendid projects greatly enriched the city's beauty. The majority of the excavated area corresponds to Hadrian's enlargement of the city (early 2nd century AD). One of the most outstanding sites is the amphitheater, the third largest in the Roman Empire with an estimated capacity of 25,000 spectators. Next to it are the mansions of the aristocracy, decorated with exquisite mosaics, in addition to the ruins of baths, temples and other buildings. The town of Santiponce boasts both the stands from the Roman theater and the monastery of **San Isidoro del Campo.**

The **Aljarafe** plateau, a hamlet of towns and haciendas (estates) nestled between olive groves, vineyards and orchards, (juts out

Itálica, casa de Neptuno (House of Neptune).

Itálica. Roman road.

Itálica. Entrances to the amphitheater.

SAN ISIDORO DEL CAMPO

Next to Santiponce is the monastery founded by Guzmán el Bueno in 1310. This jewel of Gothic-Mudejar art contains the tomb of its legendary founder – who, under siege in Tarifa, chose the death of his son over the surrender of the city – in addition to a retable with sculptures by Martinéz Montañés and various side rooms and cloisters with valuable frescos from the 15th century.

above Itálica). Its rustic character has changed since being integrated into the Sevillian metropolitan area, and it is currently a very popular area to visit and enjoy walks in the fresh air and lunch in one of its inns, restaurants or asadores (restaurants specializing in grilled and roasted meat). Among its many attractions are the prehistoric dolmens of Valencia de la Concepción; the monastery of Loreto next to Espartinas; the town of Umbrete, which has a large Baroque church and several wineries that make the famous Aljarafe wines; Olivares, the villa of the count-duke with the duke's palace and the Collegiate Church; Sanlúcar la Mayor, with its beautiful Mudejar churches and haciendas like that of Benazuza; and other unusual places like the ancient Almohad mosque of Cuatrovitas, in Bollullos.

To the south of Aljarafe, the towns of **Coria** and **Puebla del Río** (12-13 kilometers away of the SE-660 highway) mark the entrance to the **Marismas** wetlands, the fascinating landscape made up of lagoons, forests, pastures, and rice fields that follows the Guadalquivir River on its decent towards its estuary. This unlimited horizon, refuge to thousands of birds, is the site of the town of Isla Mayor,

Boat on the Guadalquivir in Coria del Río.

Carmona.

famous for its gastronomy of rice, game, crabs and other wetlands specialties, as well as Cañada de los Pájaros – a bird reservation with paths and observatories for bird watching. Other sites are the pine forests of Aznalcázar or the Abajo pastures, on the edge of the natural park that extends around

Olivares. Plaza and the Collegiate Church.

the perimeter of the Doñana National Park. Another place to visit in Coria del Río is the Moorish style house that belonged to the pioneer of Andalusian autonomy, Blas Infante.

Carmona and the Campiña (the countryside)

The gentle countryside to the east of Seville along the Guadalquivir Valley, is dotted with whitewashed towns known as pueblos blancos which have both an extraordinary monumental presence and a traditional Andalusian appearance, such as Carmona and Écija, on the edge of the A-4 freeway to Cordoba, and Marchena and Osuna, along the A-92.

Carmona (38 km), rising up in the Alcores hills, boasts one of the most important historical groupings in Andalusia. At the entrance to the city is the Roman

Carmona. Walled city.

Necropolis (1st century b.c. – 4th century a.d.), a funerary complex with hundreds of tombs dug out of the rocks. Across from the church of San Pedro and its small Giralda is the Alcázar de la Puerta de Sevilla (3rd century b.c. – 15th century), the bastion of the entrance to the walled city, a Roman, Muslim and Christian construction built on Iberian and Carthaginian foundations. The narrow cobbled streets of the historic center lead through whitewashed walls and are delightfully charming and tranquil. The plaza de San Fernando is the central point of this urban landscape. Nearby is the large church of Santa María, finished in 1518 and built on top of a mosque preserving only its courtyard, and the house of the Marques de las Torres, the location of the City Museum. The church of San Felipe, the convent of Santa Clara and many other mon-

uments lie along the sloping road leading up to the Alcázar de Arriba, the parador (typically 4 or 5 star, historic state-owned hotels) and the puerta de Córdoba, which has a panoramic view of the surrounding countryside.

Écija (94 km) is located on a shelf between cultivated fields on the banks of the Genil River. With

Necropolis at Carmona. Tomb of the Elephant.

Carmona. Patio de los Aljibes in the Alcázar de la Puerta de Sevilla.

a trio of nicknames, it is known as the "city of the sun" for its heraldic symbol, "Andalusia's frying pan", for the extreme temperatures reached during the dog days of summer, and the "city of the towers", for the forest-like arrangement of the bell towers that define its silhouette. The city combines a rich historic center with Roman and Islamic roots, with an exuberant Baroque character. Its unequivocal monumental atmosphere is breathed in upon wandering through the intricate maze of streets surrounding the plaza de España, where the number of important buildings multiplies. Palaces such as that of Peñaflor or Benamejí, currently the local museum, are two examples of some of the finest noble houses found in Andalusia, while the churches of Santa Maria, Santiago, Santa Cruz, San Juan and San Gil, with their bright towers made of brick and *azulejos* bring together a dazzling heritage of archeological finds, retables, sculptures, paintings and precious metal work.

The town of **Marchena** (60 km) is on the road to Malaga and Granada, with its Arab walls, churches like Santa María de la

Écija.

Collegiate Church of Osuna.

Collegiate Church of Osuna

The image of the town is dominated by the volume of this church, considered to be one of the most striking examples of religious architecture in the province. Such a somber construction is a faithful reflection of the enormous power of its patrons, the Duke and Duchess of Osuna, who founded it in 1535. Inside, there are magnificent retables and oil paintings by José de Ribera, and on the lower level, the incredible family mausoleum of its founders.

Mota and San Juan Bautista, which has a collection of paintings by Zurbarán, and museum dedicated to the modernist sculptor Coullaut-Valera. **Osuna** (86 km), is at the foot of a hill that has the remains of an Iberian fortress, a Roman necropolis, and the Renaissance mass that makes up the Collegiate Church. On the outskirts of town are the old University and the museum-monastery of the Encarnación, a ceramics museum whose pieces can be contemplated in the monastery's cloisters, staircases, and halls. In the lower reaches of the hill, the Arab torre del Agua (Water Tower) contains a museum dedicated to the substantial local archeology. The town of Osuna is a model of noble elegance with an atmosphere that seems to be stuck between the 16th and 18th centuries. Its long streets – San Pedro, Sevilla, de la Huerta… – line up admirable religious and noble buildings such as the palace of the Marques de la Gomera and the Cilla del Cabildo, between a careful showcase of domestic architecture with a traditional flare.

Sierra Norte of Seville

The mountains and meadows of the Sierra Norte are a sharp contrast to the plains that domi-

Marchena. Arco de la Rosa.

Guadalcanal. Church of the Asunción.

nate the majority of the province. A good place for a change of scenery, **Cazalla de la Sierra** (89 kilometers away on the A-432 highway), and the neighboring **Constantina** mark the head of this region which lies along the Sevillian length of the Sierra Morena Mountains which boasts other charming villages such as

El Pedroso, Alanís, Guadalcanal and San Nicolás del Puerto. Cazalla is a tidy whitewashed town built around the parish of the Consolación and a beautiful plaza mayor (the town's main square), as well as various convents and sunny houses which stress the ancient character of its streets. One of the loveliest spots in the surrounding areas is la Cartuja, the recovered vestiges of an ancient monastic retreat located in a marvelous wooded area surrounded by natural springs. Constantina is just as evocative, its city center located below the towers of a medieval fortress and the peaceful Moorish Quarter. Together with the incentives of its traditional heritage and nature, the Sierra Norte is renowned for its delicious local cuisine and its wonderful pork, liquors, and anises.

NATURAL PARK

167,439 hectares of the Sierra Norte of Seville has been declared a Natural Park due to the richness of its Mediterranean forests containing different varieties of oak and chestnut trees, and its interesting sites such as the Huéznar riverbank, with waterfalls and leafy trees, or the Cerro del Hierro (Iron Hill), a fantastic landscape of limestone, hollowed out by erosion and mining. The Robledo, on the outskirts of Constantina, serves as the visitor center for this protected area.

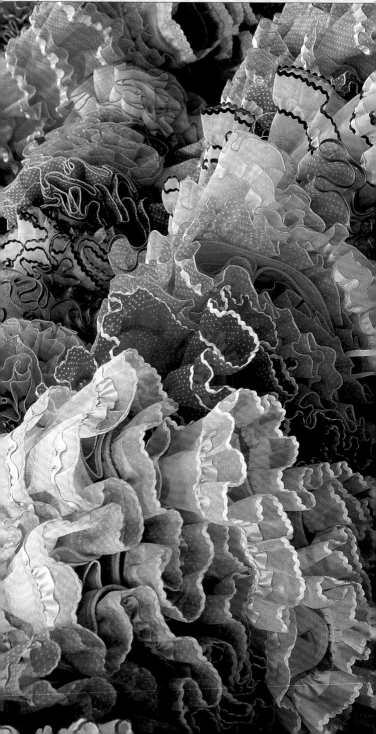

Practical Guide

LEISURE ACTIVITIES

Seville has the well deserved reputation for being one of the most festive cities in Spain. Its fiestas have a noted repercussion on the rhythm of life and the city's appearance, because for Sevillians, the street is both a fundamental medium for socializing, and the most popular stage for the city's celebrations. Although winter and fall are not lacking in festivities, spring is by far the most festive season. While many of the festivals have religious roots, their magnitude and connotations allow them to transcend the religious and become something to be enjoyed by all.

FIESTAS

Parade of the Three Wise Men
5 of January. The favorite parade of children. It leaves from the parque María Luisa and follows a long route through the city.

Andalusia Day
28 of February. Holiday of the Autonomous Community.

Semana Santa (Holy Week)
March-April. The enormous festival makes the city come alive with people. It includes dozens of processions (floats) and canopies carried by costaleros and escorted by Nazarenes, from Palm Sunday to Easter Sunday, or the day of the Resurrection. Each of the different paths have the Official Route in common, the route flanked by observation boxes and chairs that goes

from La Campana down calle Sierpes, to the plaza de San Francisco and avenida de la Constitución to the Cathedral. La Madrugá (early morning) – from Thursday to Holy Friday – is the culminating moment of Semana Santa in Seville, when it is the turn for the processions of the brotherhoods of Jesús del Gran Poder and the Macarena, among others.

Feria de Abril (April Festival)
The most important secular fiesta in Seville takes place one or two weeks after Semana Santa at which time the Real de la Feria, an ephemeral city of tents and amusement park rides next to the neighborhood of Los Remedios, comes to life. It begins at midnight on Monday with the lighting of the entrance gate. Riders and horse-drawn carriages pass through the grounds, their occupants singing Andalusian folk songs, and the festivities continue day and night throughout the week. The Feria de Abril was founded in 1847 as a livestock market. Since then, it has become more and more festive every year.

Cruces de Mayo
(Crosses of May)
Starts the 3rd of May. Courtyards and plazas in the City Center – around San Vicente, Santa Catalina, etc – are adorned with crosses, altars, flowers and hanging tapestries and are used as sites for gatherings and fiestas.

San Fernando
May 30th. Local celebration. The body of the patron Saint of Seville is put on display in the Cathedral.

Romería del Rocío
(Pilgrimage)
At the end of May, beginning of June. Various brotherhoods carrying banners called "simpecados" and horse drawn carriages leave Seville and begin a pilgrimage to the hermitage of the Rocío, in Almonte (Huelva). The departure is a sight to see.

Corpus Christi
Held on a Thursday at the end of May or the beginning of June. According to tradition it is one of the three sunniest Thursdays in the year. The procession followed by the Corpus is decorated with altars, hanging tapestries and plants. The Custodia's entourage leaves the Cathedral very early Thursday morning.

Velá of Santa Ana
Around the 25th of July, this is the most important celebration in the Triana district. Held in the plaza del Altozano and

Feria de Abril.

Trajes de flamenca (Flamenco dresses).

Corpus Christi.

calle Betis which are decorated with lights, stages, tents, and kiosks. There are contests – such as the "greasy pole" in the river – and performances.

Virgen de los Reyes
August 15th. Holiday of the patron saint of Seville. Leaves the Cathedral first thing in the morning as part of a procession that circles the building.

Inmaculada Concepción
December 8. On the eve of this day a crowd gathers in front of the monument of the Inmaculada in the plaza del Triunfo. The following day in the Cathedral there is a performance of the old dance of the "seises", children that sing and dance in front of the Main Altar.

New Year's Eve
December 31st. Every year more and more people attend the countdown to midnight in the plaza Nueva, in front of the City Hall's clock.

BULLS AND FLAMENCO
The bullfighting tradition in Seville is one of the first in Spain. The early bull events were held in the plaza de San Francisco and, later, in the wooden enclosures of the Arenal, until the current bullring was built in the middle of the 18th century. Visits to the Maestranza bullring and its

Bullfighting Museum are a very informative way to learn about bullfighting in Seville and the history of tauromachy. The season begins on Easter Sunday and lasts until the end of the Feria. Then on there are Sunday bullfights, special bullfights for the Corpus, for the feria de San Miguel, to the end of September, and the season officially ends on the 12th of October.

Seville is also one of the essential stages for the art of Flamenco, which has an especially long tradition. In addition to performances in theaters, flamenco bars, clubs, and cafes, the Flamenco Biennial held during September in even-numbered years, is one of the most important festivals of this genre.

MUSEUMS

Andalusian Center for Contemporary Art
Conjunto Monumental de la Cartuja.
Avenida Américo Vespucio, 2.
Tel. 955 03 70 70
www.juntadeandalucia.es/cultura/caac

Archeological Museum
Plaza de América n/n
Tel. 954 23 24 01
www.juntadeandalucia.es/cultura/museoarqueologicosevilla

Museum of Art and Local Customs
Plaza de América, 3
Tel. 954 23 25 76
www.juntadeandalucia.es/cultura/museoartesycostumbrespopularessevilla

Museum of Fine Arts
Plaza del Museo, 9
Tel. 954 22 50 84
www.juntadeandalucia.es/cultura/museobellasartessevilla

Carriage Museum
Convent of los Remedios
Plaza de Cuba n/n
Tel. 954 27 26 04
www.museodecarruajes.com

Cathedral Museum
Cathedral
Plaza Virgen de los Reyes n/n
Tel. 954 21 49 71

Maritime Museum
Torre del Oro
Paseo de Cristóbal Colón n/n.
Tel. 954 22 24 19

Museum of Santa Paula
Calle Santa Paula, 11
Tel. 954 53 63 30

Museum Palace of Lebrija
Calle Cuna, 8
Tel. 954 22 78 02
www.palaciodelebrija.com

Bullfighting Museum
Plaza de toros de la Maestranza
(Maestanza Bull Ring)
Paseo de Cristóbal Colón, 12
Tel. 954 21 03 15
www.realmaestranza.com

Plaza de América and Museum of Arts and Local Customs.

PERFORMANCES

Teatro Central
Theater and contemporary music.
Calle José de Gálvez n/n
Isla de la Cartuja
Tel. 955 03 72 00
www.teatrocentral.com

Teatro Lope de Vega
Stage art, music.
Avenida de María Luisa n/n
Tel. 954 59 08 67

Teatro de la Maestranza
Classical music, opera, ballet, other music.
Paseo de Colón, 22
Tel. 954 22 33 44
www.teatromaestranza.com

Office of the Flamenco Biennial
Up to date information on performances, festivals, and flamenco shows. The Flamenco Biennial of Seville is held in several different venues throughout the city.

Pabellón Real
Plaza de América n/n
Tel. 954 59 28 70
www.bienal-flamenco.org

SEVILLE FOR CHILDREN

Isla Mágica
Theme park inspired by Seville's Golden Age, with recreations of the city's port, Caribbean castles and pirate ships. Attractions for all ages. Open from April through the beginning of November.
Isla de la Cartuja n/n
Entrance next to the puente (bridge) de la Barqueta.
Tel. 902 16 17 16

Parque de María Luisa
(María Luisa Park)
Walking through the plaza de España, taking a ride on a bicycle or a four wheel "cycles", or feeding the pigeons in the plaza de América, are all fun activities for children in the park.

PRACTICAL INFORMATION

TRANSPORTATION

BY AIR

San Pablo Airport
Highway A-4, km 532 (7 km)
Tel. 954 44 90 00
In addition to fixed rates taxis, there is a bus service that runs between the airport and the city center, its final stop next to the puerta de Jerez. It operates between 6:15 or 6:45am depending on the day of the week, and 11:00 at night, with buses leaving in either direction every half hour. The trajectory takes around 20-30 minutes, depending on traffic.
Tel. 900 71 01 71 and 954 44 91 28
www.aena.es

BY TRAIN

Santa Justa Station
Avenida de Kansas City n/n
Tel. 954 41 41 11 and 954 53 76 26
All of the train lines including the AVE and Cercanías (commuter) trains.

Renfe (National Train Network)

AVE (Spanish High Speed Train)
Tel. 902 24 02 02
www.renfe.es
www.eltren.com

BY BUS

Plaza de Armas Station
Buses to el Aljarafe, towns to the west of Seville, Huelva, Portugal, Extremadura, Madrid, Barcelona, Northern Spain, and other European countries.
Tel. 954 90 80 40

Prado de San Sebastián Station
Buses to the majority of towns in the province of Seville (Carmona, Écija, etc.) provinces of Cadiz, Cordoba, Granada, Malaga, Jaén and Almería.
Tel. 954 41 71 11

City Buses
The local bus network has over 50 lines that cover the city in its entirety and its outskirts as far as the airport. Buses circulate daily from 6 am to 23:15–23:45 pm, or 23:45–24:00 in the summer months. The six lines of the night bus leave from the plaza Nueva at midnight, 1am and 2am.

TUSSAM (Sevillian Urban Municipal Transport)
Tel. 900 71 01 71 and 902 45 99 54
Lost and Found:
Tel. 954 42 04 03
www.tussam.es

TAXIS

Tele-Taxi Sevilla
Tel. 954 62 22 22

Radio Taxi
Tel. 954 58 00 00

Radio Taxi Giralda
Tel. 954 67 55 55

USEFUL TELEPHONE NUMBERS

Government of Andalusia
Tel. 902 50 55 05

Tourist Office of the Government of Andalusia
Avenida de la Constitución, 21 Tel. 954 22 14 04

Tourist Office of the Seville City Hall
Laredo Building
Plaza de San Francisco, 19

Tel: 954 59 52 88
Naves del Barranco
Calle Arjona, 28
Tel. 954 22 17 14 and
902 19 48 97
Tourist Office of the Seville City Council
Plaza del Triunfo, 1
Tel. 954 21 00 05
Information about Seville
Tel. 010
Telephone information
Tel. 11888
Emergencies
Tel. 112
Medical emergencies
Tel. 061
Police
Tel. 091 y 092
Late night pharmacies
Tel. 902 52 21 11

SEVILLE ON THE WEB

www.sevilla.org
Seville City Hall
www.turismo.sevilla.org
Webpage of the Seville Consortium of Tourism
www.juntadeandalucia.es
Webpage for Andalusia
www.andalucia.org

WHERE TO SLEEP

Hotel Alfonso XIII [★★★★★]
Luxury hotel in a monumental building, regional style with a colonial flare.
Calle San Fernando, 2
Tel. 954 91 70 00

Hotel Casa Imperial [★★★★★]
A delicious palace from the Golden Age behind the Casa de Pilatos.
Calle Imperial, 29
Tel. 954 50 03 00
Hotel Bécquer [★★★★]
Convenient quality and location at the entrance to the City Center.
Calle Reyes Católicos, 4
Tel. 954 22 89 00
Hotel Las Casas del Rey de Baeza [★★★★]
A group of restored houses in the heart of the historic City Center.
Plaza Jesús de la Redención, 2
Tel. 954 56 14 96
Hotel Meliá Sevilla [★★★★]
Functional and spacious, next to the parque María Luisa.
Calle Pedro de Castro, 1
Tel. 954 42 15 11
Hotel Rey Alfonso X [★★★★]
Modern hotel contrasting with the historic atmosphere of the Jewish Quarter
Calle Ximénez de Enciso, 35
Tel. 954 21 00 70
Hotel Sevilla Center [★★★★]
One of the highest and most modern buildings in Seville, located in a tower in the Buhaira Gardens.
Avenida de la Buhaira n/n
Tel. 954 54 95 00
Hotel Vincci La Rábida [★★★★]
House and courtyard restored

Hotel Alfonso XIII.

with exquisite care.
Calle Castelar, 24
Tel. 954 50 12 80
Hotel Las Casas de la Judería [★★★]
Attractive collection of courtyards and restored houses.
Santa María la Blanca-Callejón de Dos Hermanas, 7
Tel. 954 41 51 50
Hotel San Gil [★★★★]
In the style of a modernist mansion, close to the Macarena.
Calle Parras, 28
Tel. 954 90 68 11
Hotel Las Casas de los Mercaderes [★★★]
Next to el Salvador, a traditional building, with all of the amenities.
Calle Álvarez Quintero, 9
Tel. 954 22 58 58
Hotel NH Plaza de Armas [★★★]
A modern and practical hotel at the edge of the City Center.
Calle Marqués de Paradas n/n
Tel. 954 90 19 92
Hotel Amadeus [★★]
A musical theme hotel in the Santa Cruz district.
Calle Farnesio, 6.
Tel. 954 50 14 43
Hotel Simón [★]
Pleasant large house around a courtyard, close to the Cathedral.
Calle García de Vinuesa, 19.
Tel. 954 22 66 60

Plaza de Refinadores.

Hostal Monreal
Affordable and very conveniently located in the Santa Cruz district.
Calle Rodrigo Caro, 8
Tel. 954 21 41 66

Hostal Sierpes
Simple and economical in the City Center.
Calle Corral del Rey, 22
Tel. 954 22 49 48

Albergue Juvenil
Youth hostel near the park.
Calle Isaac Peral, 2
Tel. 954 61 31 50

Andalusia Tourism information and reservations.
Tel. 902 20 00 037

Seville Hotel Association
Tel. 954 22 15 38
www.hotelesdesevilla.com

Infhor, Seville hotels
Tel. 954 54 19 52

EATING AND DRINKING

GOURMET DINING

Egaña Oriza
Northern cuisine, next to the Alcázar.
Calle San Fernando, 41
Tel. 954 22 72 11

La Alquería
The art of Ferrán Adriá in Southern lands, in the somber ambience of an Aljarafe hacienda.

Hacienda Benazuza
Calle Virgen de las Nieves n/n
Sanlúcar la Mayor
Tel. 955 70 33 44

CLASSIC RESTAURANTS

Casa Robles
Next to the Cathedral, a traditional Sevillian restaurant.
Calle Álvarez Quintero, 58
Tel. 954 56 32 72

Enrique Becerra
Faithfully prepareed traditional recipes. Just a few steps away from plaza Nueva.
Calle Gamazo, 2
Tel. 954 21 30 49

La Isla
Fish and meat specialties.

Calle Arfe, 25
Tel. 954 21 26 21

La Judería
Close to the jardines de Murillo, serving excellent fish and shellfish.
Calle Cano y Cueto, 13
Tel. 954 41 20 52

RESTAURANTS

Az-zait
An original restaurant serving Mediterranean cuisine.
Plaza de San Lorenzo, 1
Tel. 954 90 64 75

Eslava
Pioneer of modern cuisine with a cozy atmosphere next to the plaza de San Lorenzo.
Calle Eslava, 3
Tel. 954 90 65 68

Casablanca
For sitting at a table or having tapas at the bar, with specialties of the house and traditional dishes.
Calle Zaragoza, 50
Tel. 954 22 46 98

La Albahaca
Located in a sumptuous house-palace in the Santa Cruz district.
Plaza de Santa Cruz, 9.
Tel. 954 22 07 14

Poncio
Innovative cooking in Triana.
Calle Victoria, 8
Tel. 954 34 00 10

Sabina
In a grand restored house in

Arenal, convenient location and pleasant service.
Calle Dos de Mayo, 4
Tel. 945 56 25 47

Salvador Rojo
Contemporary menu and décor. Calle San Fernando, 3
Tel. 954 22 97 25

San Marco
Popular and affordable Italian restaurant chain in the Santa Cruz district.

District of Santa Cruz.

Calle Mesón del Moro, 6
Tel. 954 56 43 90

Taberna del Alabardero
Close to the plaza Nueva, it combines modernity and tradition.
Calle Zaragoza, 20
Tel. 954 56 06 37

TAPAS

Bar Estrella
Quiet and tranquil, in a corner of the City Center.
Calle Estrella, 3
Tel. 954 22 75 35

Calle Sierpes. Bar Laredo.

Typical products to prepare traditional recipes.

La Alicantina
Plaza del Salvador, 2
Tel. 954 22 61 22

Casa Cuesta
An essential stop on a tapas
tour of Triana.
Calle Castilla, 1
Tel. 954 33 33 35

Bar Giralda
One of the largest selections
of tapas, in the shadow of
the Giralda.
Calle Mateos Gago, 1
Tel. 954 22 74 35

Barbiana
Specialties from Sanlúcar de
Barrameda, fish and
shellfish.
Calle Albareda, 11
Tel. 954 21 12 39

Becerrita
Traditional Sevillian cuisine
in a historic establishment.
Calle Recaredo, 9
Tel. 954 53 37 27

Bodega Góngora
A very popular meeting point,
next to the plaza Nueva.
Calle Albareda, 5
Tel. 21 11 19

Casa Ricardo
Intimate atmosphere, next to
San Lorenzo.
Calle Hernán Cortés, 2.
Tel. 954 38 97 51

Casa Román
Cozy with delicious pork products, in the Santa Cruz district. Plaza de los Venerables,
1. Tel 954 22 84 83

El Rinconcillo
The oldest tavern in Seville.
Calle Gerona, 40
Tel. 954 22 31 83

La Trastienda
Fresh ingredients and imagi-
nation served up as tapas.
Calle Alfalfa, 8
Tel. 954 22 69 26

Modesto
Very busy, with an outside
terrace in front of the
jardínes Murillo.
Calle Cano y Cueto, 5
Tel. 954 41 68 11

El Cairo
Quality establishment on the
way to the puente de Triana.
Calle Reyes Católicos, 13
Tel. 954 21 30 89

Mesón Cinco Jotas
In el Arenal, the cerdo ibérico
(Iberian pork) is king.
Calle Castelar, 1 on the cor-
ner of Arfe
Tel. 954 21 58 62

Las Teresas
With all of the character of
the Santa Cruz district.
Calle Santa Teresa, 2
Tel. 954 21 30 69

Manolo León
In a large modernish house
near San Lorenzo.
Calle Guadalquivir, 12
Tel. 954 37 37 35

Sol y Sombra
At the limits of Triana,
conserves the essence of
favorite tapas and raciones

(larger portions).
Calle Castilla, 151
Tel. 954 33 39 35

SEVILLE AT NIGHT

The climate and traditions
of Seville are part of the
motives for the city's intense
and lively night life. The
many areas with tapas bars
– in the vicinity of the
Cathedral, Santa Cruz, la
Alfalfa, around the plaza
Nueva, el Salvador, San
Lorenzo, el Arenal, Triana
and other periphery neighborhoods – are bustling with
people until all hours, especially after Thursdays. The
outside terraces in the gardens and parks also attract
large crowds – el Prado, la
Buhaira, las Delicias and
the plaza de América,
Triana, la Cartuja –. Late
night bars abound in the
Alfalfa, Arenal, Troneo, the
Cartuja, Alameda de
Hércules, and in general all
over the City Center.

FLAMENCO

In addition to performances
during festivals and in theaters, flamenco can be seen
performed in tablaos (traditional flamenco bars) and
other informal places such
as tapas bars and outdoor
terraces where there are

Tablao flamenco.

sporadic performances, such
as in Casa Anselma and La
Carbonería.
Casa Anselma
Calle Pagés del Corro, 49
Tel. 954 33 40 03
El Arenal. Tablao
Calle Rodo, 7
Tel. 954 21 64 92
Los Gallos. Tablao
Plaza de Santa Cruz, 11
Tel. 954 21 69 81
Sol Café Cantante
Calle Sol, 5
Tel. 954 22 51 65
La Carbonería
Calle Levíes, 18
Tel. 954 56 37 55

SHOPPING AREAS

In the City Center, between
the plazas Nueva, la
Magdalena and el Duque,
there is a large shopping
area in the area around
calles Tetuán, Rioja, and
Sierpes among others. There
are both modern and
traditional stores as well as
department stores. Towards
el Salvador and calle Francos
there are many stores selling
traditional Sevillian wares
(mantones or embroidered
shawls, fans, hats, shoes and
other leather goods). The
Santa Cruz district has sou-
venir shops and in Triana,
ceramics. In the los
Remedios neighborhood there
is an important shopping
area along the calle
Asunción, while Nervión
boasts the most modern and
bustling places to shop.
STORES
El Torno
Artisan pastries made by
cloistered nuns.
Plaza del Cabildo n/n
Tel. 954 21 91 90
Cerámica Santa Ana
Traditional pottery from
Triana.

Tienda de ceramicas. Barrio de Triana

Calle San Jorge, 31
Tel. 954 33 39 90
Populart
Ceramics, crafts, and other
traditional objects
Pasaje de Vila, 4
Tel. 954 22 94 44
El Caballo
Leather and fur items, fash-
ion, equestrian and hunting
goods.
Calle Antonia Díaz, 7
Tel. 954 21 81 27
Feliciano Foronda
Mantones de Manila.
(Embroidered Shawls)
Calle Álvarez Quintero, 52
Tel. 954 22 91 48
J. Foronda
Mantones, mantillas (lace),
accessories.
Calle Tetuán, 28
Tel. 954 22 60 60
Lina
Trajes de flamenca.
(Flamenco dresses)
Calle Lineros, 17
Tel. 954 21 24 23
Maquedano
Hats.
Calle Sierpes, 40
Tel. 954 56 47 71
Casa del Libro
Books. Calle Velázquez, 8
Tel. 954 50 29 50
Librería Beta
Books.
Calle Sagasta, 16
Tel. 954 22 84 95
SPANISH BRANDS
In the City Center (plaza
Nueva and most importantly

calles Tetuán, Rioja and
Sierpes) there are stores for
the brands Loewe, Camper,
Zara, Adolfo Domínguez,
Purificación García,
Caramelo and other fashion
and accessory franchises.
STREET MARKETS
El Jueves
Calle Feria. The oldest one
in Seville, bargain items,
curiosity goods, Thursday
mornings.
Collector's items
Plaza del Cabildo, next to the
avenida de la Constitución.
Coins, stamps, post cards
and other collector's items.
Sunday mornings.
Animals
Plaza de la Alfalfa. All kinds
of pets. Sunday mornings.
Paintings
Plaza del Museo. Oils, draw-
ings, and graphic art, mostly
with a Sevillian theme, by
local and young artists.
Sunday mornings.

FAIRS AND CONFERENCES

Fibes
Conference and Exposition
Center of Seville
Avenida Alcalde Luis
Uruñuela n/n.
Tel. 954 47 87 00
Modern structure with large
pavilions and a striking
gold dome. Used for fairs,
conferences and other
events. Located in the east-
ern part of the city, very
close to the SE-30. Some of
the fairs celebrated here
include: the World
Bullfighting Fair, in
February; the World
Flamenco Festival, in
September, and the SICAB,
International Horse Fair, the
largest fair dedicated to the
equestrian world, in
November. www.fibes.es.

Index

We would like to acknowledge the collaboration of all entities
and people who have made this edition possible.

Published by: Ediciones Aldeasa
Editorial Coordination: Carmen de Francisco

Text: Fernando Olmedo
Translation from Spanish: Adrienne Smith
Photographs:
Archivo Ediciones Aldeasa: pages 7, 8, 12, 14a, 16b, 17b,
18a, 18b, 19, 20, 21, 22b, 24b-25b, 26-27, 28, 29a, 29b,
33b, 44b, 48-49a, 49b, 50, 51a, 51b, 55a, 55b, 86, 87,
88a and 92a.
José Barea: pages 9, 10-11a, 15a, 23a, 32-33a, 33c, 34a,
34b, 35a, 36, 37b, 38, 39a, 39b, 42a, 42b, 43a, 45a, 52a,
52b, 53a, 53c, 56, 57b, 57c, 58, 60a-61, 62a, 63a, 63b,
64a, 65a, 66, 68, 71b, 73b, 74a and 91a.
Hidalgo-Lopesino: pages 4, 6, 11b, 14b-15b, 16a-17a, 22a,
23b, 25c, 30, 35b, 37a, 40, 41a, 41b, 43b, 45b, 46, 53b,
54, 57a, 60b, 62b, 65b, 67a, 70, 71a, 72a, 72b, 73a, 74b,
75, 76, 78a-79a, 78b, 79a, 79b, 81a, 82a, 82b, 83a, 88b,
90a, 90b, 91b, 92b and 93.
César Justel: pages 44a, 80, 81b, 83b, 84, 85a and 85b.
Iberimage: page 67b.
Cover photograph: José Barea, a, b. Archivo Aldeasa, c.

Graphic Design: Estudio OdZ
Layout: Mariana Grekoff
Cartography: Pedro Monzo
Typeset: Cromotex
Printed by: Brizzolis

© Ediciones Aldeasa, 2006
© of the photographs: Archivo Ediciones Aldeasa
ISBN: 84-8003-527-7
ISBN: 978-84-8003-527-9
Depósito Legal: M-2756-2006
Printed in Spain